JUSTIN DELLO JOIO
DUE PER DUE
FOR VIOLONCELLO AND PIANO

I. Elegia – to an Old Musician

II. Moto Perpetuo

Duration: *ca.* 13 minutes

Commissioned for cellist Carter Brey
by the Barlow Endowment for Music Composition

ISBN 978-1-4584-7106-2

EDWARD B.
MARKS MUSIC
COMPANY /  EXCLUSIVELY DISTRIBUTED BY
HAL•LEONARD®
CORPORATION
7777 W. BLUEMOUND RD. P.O. BOX 13819 MILWAUKEE, WI 53213

www.ebmarks.com
www.halleonard.com

World Premiere given on December 19, 2010
by Carter Brey, cello, and Christopher O'Riley, piano
at Dreyfoos Hall, the Kravis Center for the Performing Arts, West Palm Beach, Florida

PROGRAM NOTE

I wrote *Due per Due* for cellist, Carter Brey, after having the privilege of his recording and premiering my *Music for Piano Trio* ("*The March of Folly*"), and I was thrilled when I learned that the pianist Christopher O'Riley would join him in premiering it.

The first of the two movements, "Elegia – to an Old Musician" has a personal aspect to it. As a six year old, I played a piano piece entitled "Prelude – to a Young Musician" by my father, Norman, which I thought was very lovely. Although that prelude was not written for me, I borrowed the idea of the title when I wrote an elegy for him, after he recently passed away at age 95. The opening section is a dark, mournful melody, heard over a sustained open cello string and an aleatoric accompaniment. A simple lyrical section and variation follow, that for me recalls the moving lyricism in my father's work. The music reaches toward an emotional climax, but fails when it is interrupted by the return of the music of the first part, and descends into a dark cadence.

The second movement, "Moto Perpetuo," is a virtuosic piece, inspired by something marvelous I heard Mr. Brey casually playing while warming up for the recording sessions for my Piano Trio. The sound of a virtuoso never fails to give me great pleasure. After having just completed a one-act opera (*Blue Mountain*) about the final days of the aged composer Edvard Grieg, and then composing this first movement elegy, I wanted to write a second movement that is a fun, technical showpiece.

Justin Dello Joio

Cover drawing by Andrew DeVries

Commissioned by the Barlow Endowment
—to Carter Brey—

DUE PER DUE

Justin Dello Joio

I. Elegia — to an Old Musician

* begin arco imperceptibly, no break in glissando and sound

** + = dampen string at the bridge, ∘ = release finger from string immediately after note is struck.

Copyright © 2009 by Piedmont Music Company
Sole Selling Agent: Edward B. Marks Music Company
All Rights Reserved   International Copyright Secured   Printed in the U.S.A.

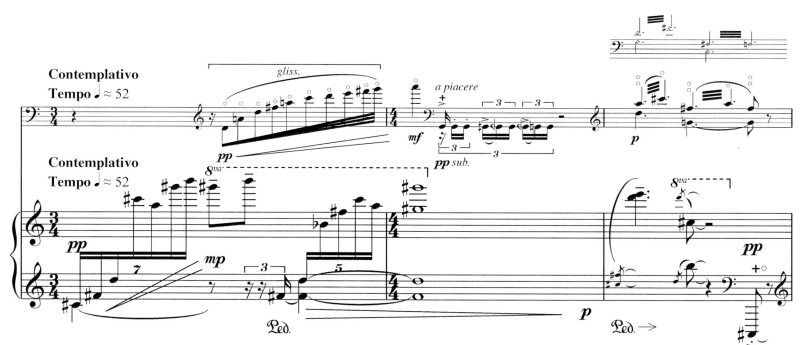

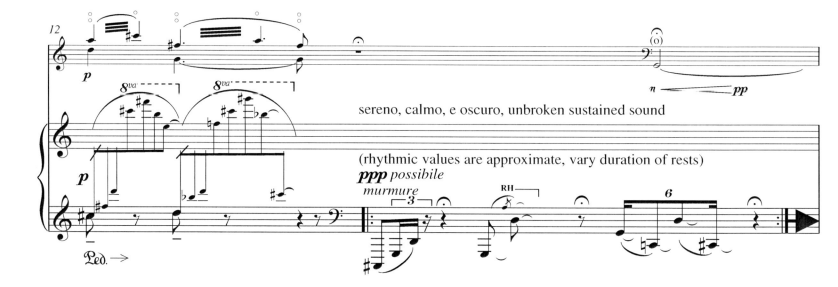

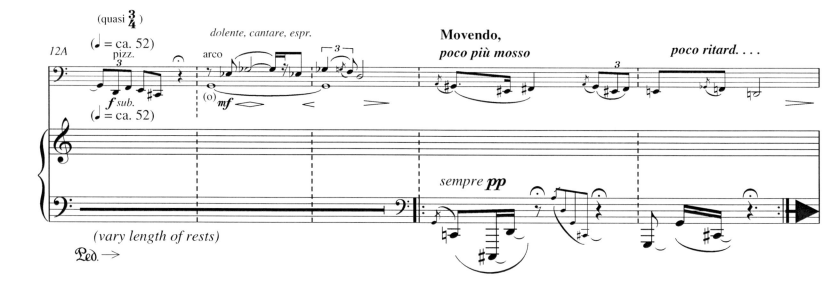

(chords in the upper system of piano in treble clef and the cello are played rhythmically in meter;
the LH piano pattern continues ad libitum)

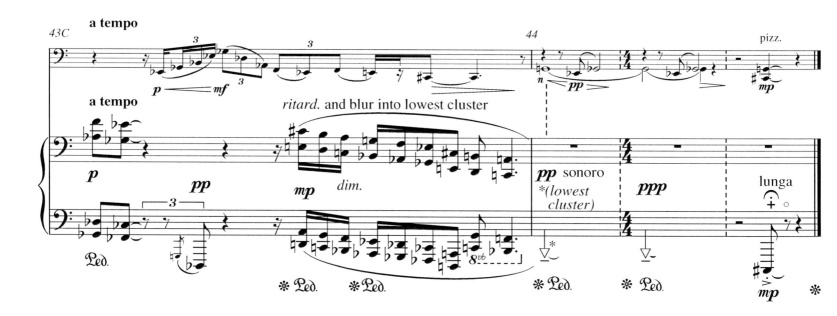

II. Moto Perpetuo

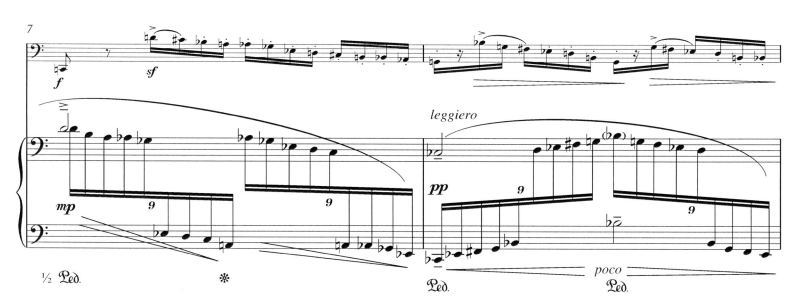

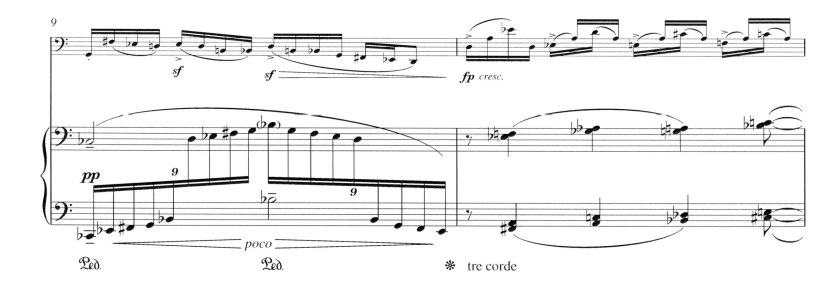

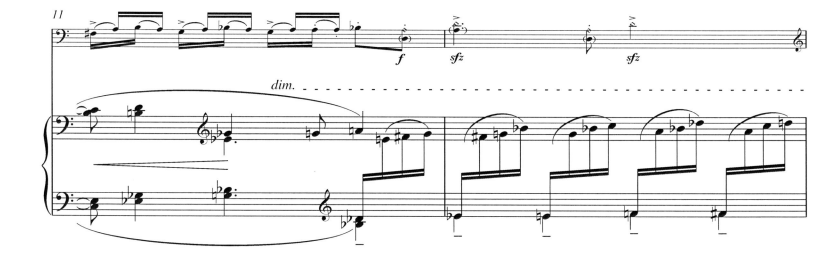

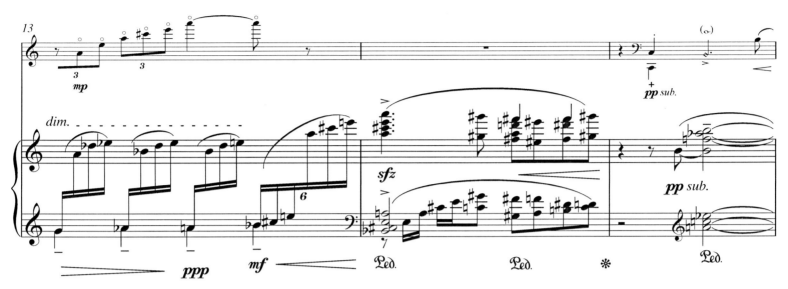

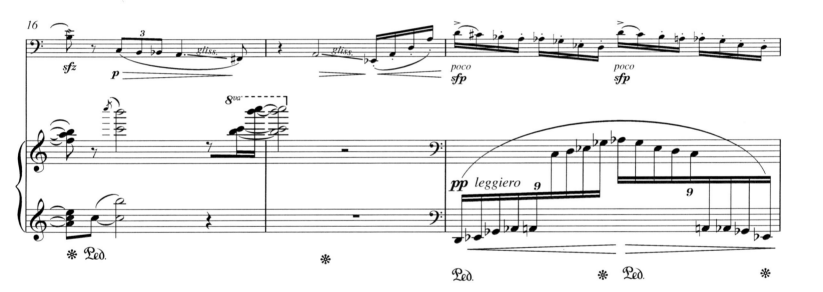

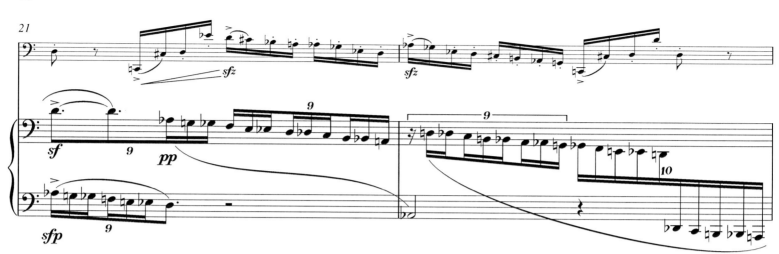

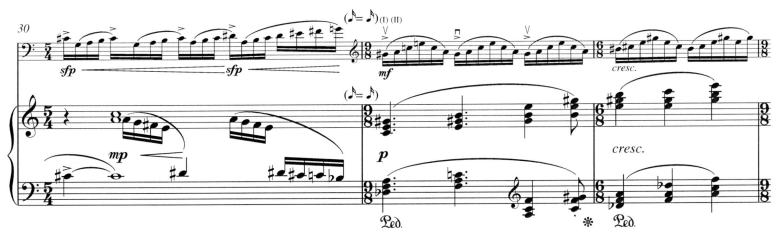

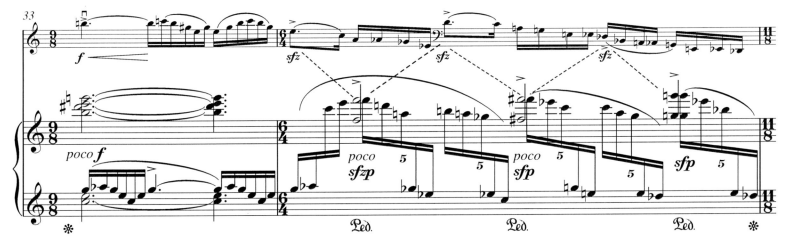

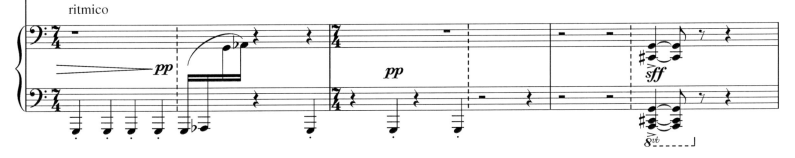

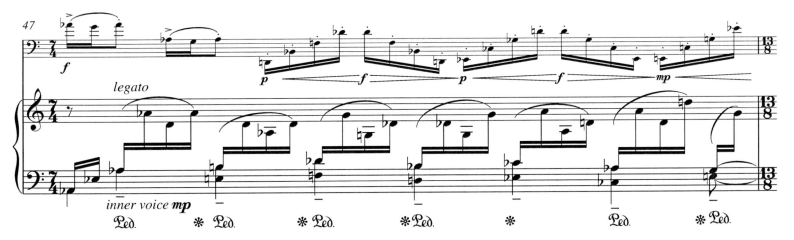

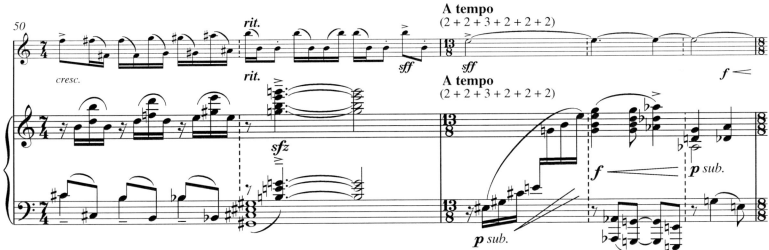

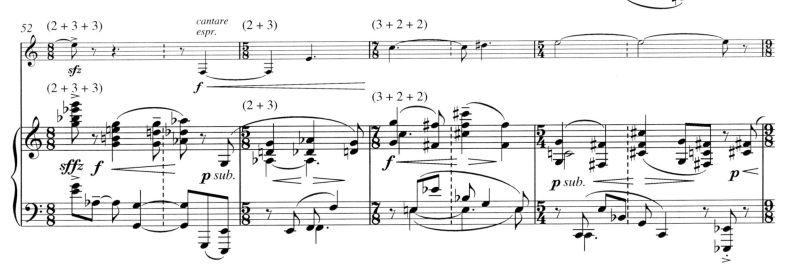

VIOLONCELLO

JUSTIN DELLO JOIO
DUE PER DUE
FOR VIOLONCELLO AND PIANO

I. Elegia – to an Old Musician

II. Moto Perpetuo

Duration: *ca.* 13 minutes

Commissioned for cellist Carter Brey
by the Barlow Endowment for Music Composition

ISBN 978-1-4584-7106-2

EDWARD B.
MARKS MUSIC
COMPANY / EXCLUSIVELY DISTRIBUTED BY
HAL•LEONARD®
CORPORATION
7777 W. BLUEMOUND RD. P.O. BOX 13819 MILWAUKEE, WI 53213

www.ebmarks.com
www.halleonard.com

World Premiere given on December 19, 2010
by Carter Brey, cello, and Christopher O'Riley, piano
at Dreyfoos Hall, the Kravis Center for the Performing Arts, West Palm Beach, Florida

PROGRAM NOTE

I wrote *Due per Due* for cellist, Carter Brey, after having the privilege of his recording and premiering my *Music for Piano Trio* ("*The March of Folly*"), and I was thrilled when I learned that the pianist Christopher O'Riley would join him in premiering it.

The first of the two movements, "Elegia – to an Old Musician" has a personal aspect to it. As a six year old, I played a piano piece entitled "Prelude – to a Young Musician" by my father, Norman, which I thought was very lovely. Although that prelude was not written for me, I borrowed the idea of the title when I wrote an elegy for him, after he recently passed away at age 95. The opening section is a dark, mournful melody, heard over a sustained open cello string and an aleatoric accompaniment. A simple lyrical section and variation follow, that for me recalls the moving lyricism in my father's work. The music reaches toward an emotional climax, but fails when it is interrupted by the return of the music of the first part, and descends into a dark cadence.

The second movement, "Moto Perpetuo," is a virtuosic piece, inspired by something marvelous I heard Mr. Brey casually playing while warming up for the recording sessions for my Piano Trio. The sound of a virtuoso never fails to give me great pleasure. After having just completed a one-act opera (*Blue Mountain*) about the final days of the aged composer Edvard Grieg, and then composing this first movement elegy, I wanted to write a second movement that is a fun, technical showpiece.

Justin Dello Joio

Violoncello

Commissioned by the Barlow Endowment
—to Carter Brey—

DUE PER DUE

I. Elegia — to an Old Musician

Justin Dello Joio

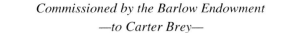

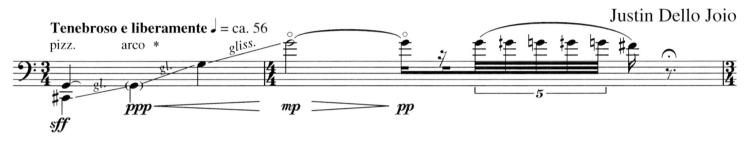

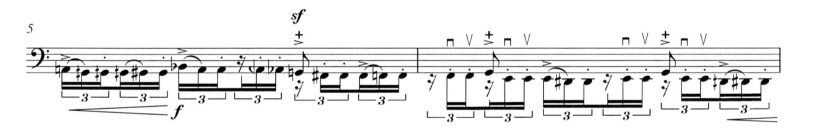

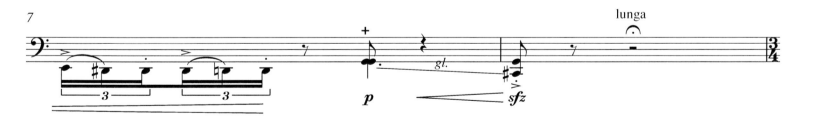

Copyright © 2009 by Piedmont Music Company
Sole Selling Agent: Edward B. Marks Music Company
All Rights Reserved   International Copyright Secured   Printed in the U.S.A.

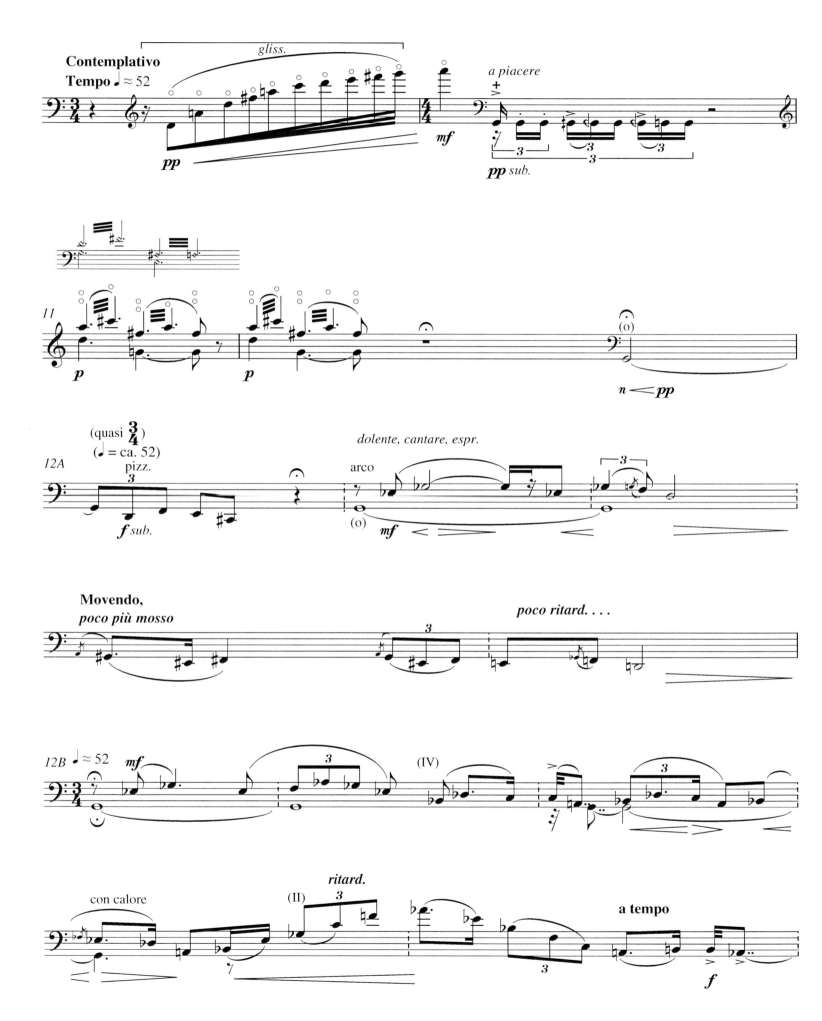

Blank for page turn

II. Moto Perpetuo

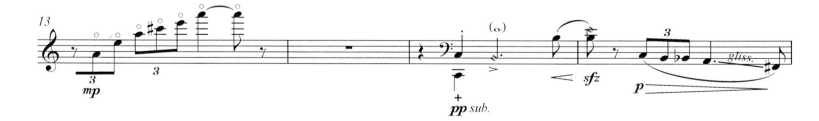

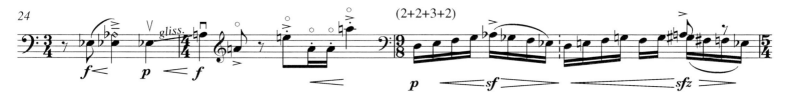

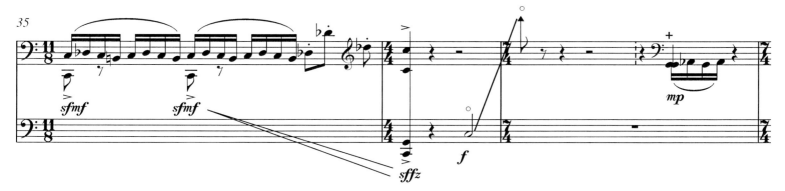

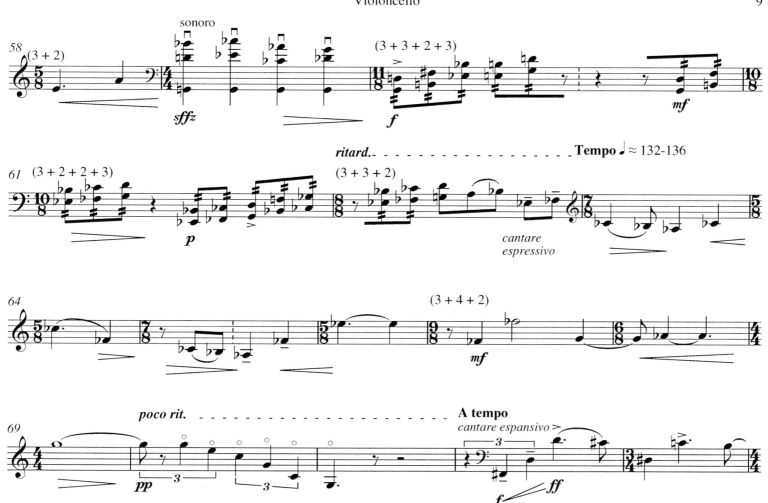

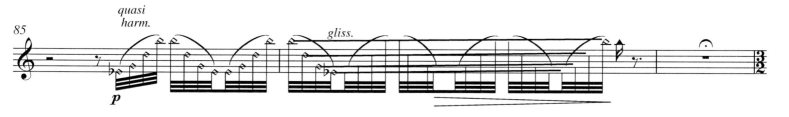

Violoncello

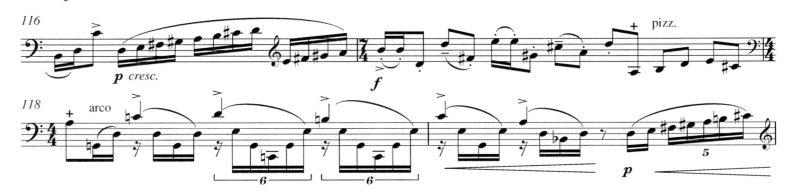

Violoncello

192

195

197

199

202

205

207

209

212

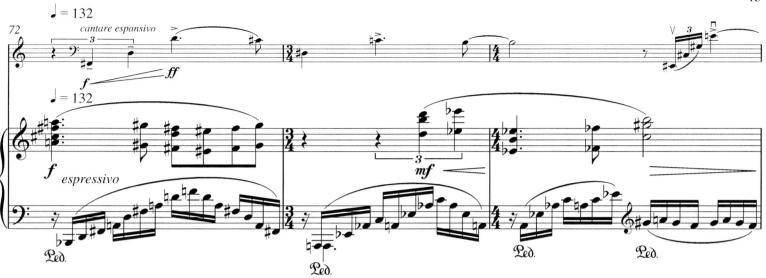

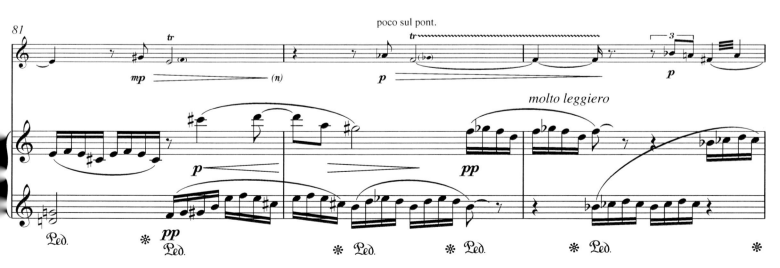

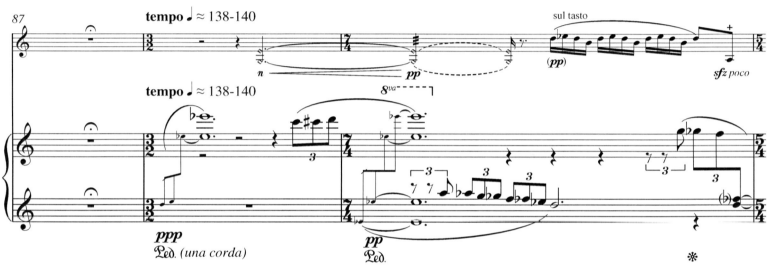

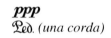

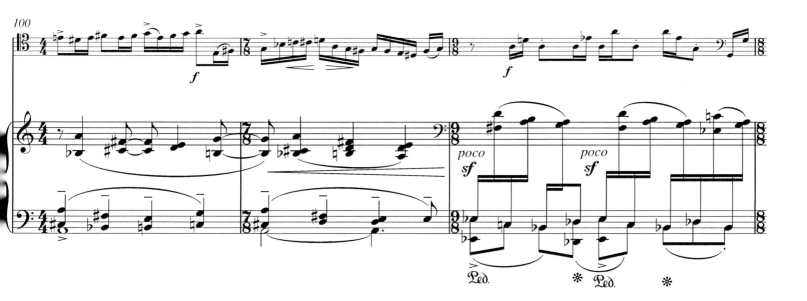

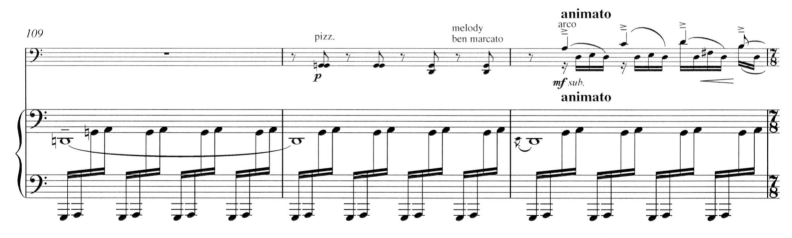

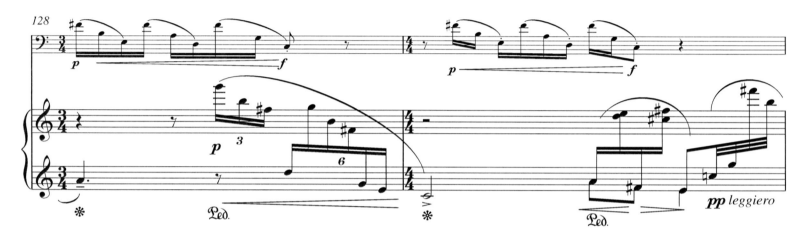

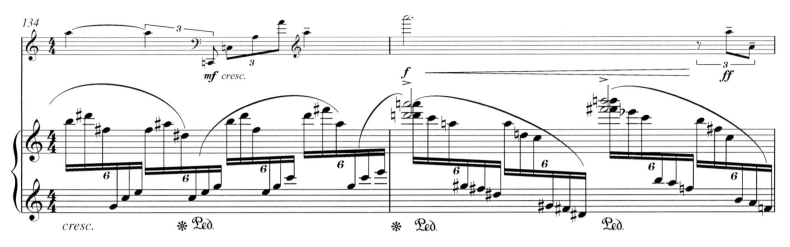

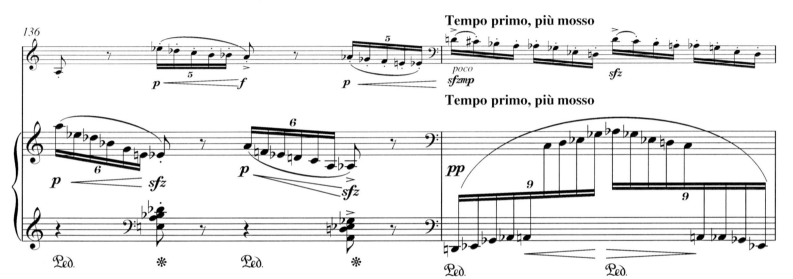

Tempo primo, più mosso

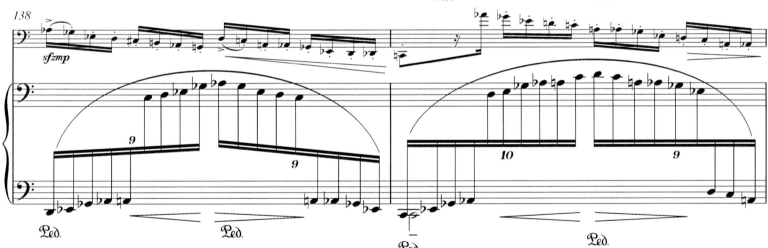

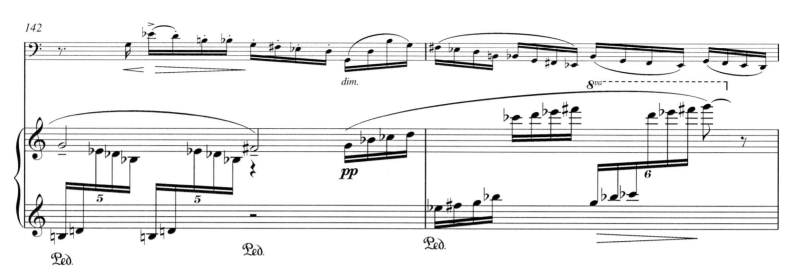

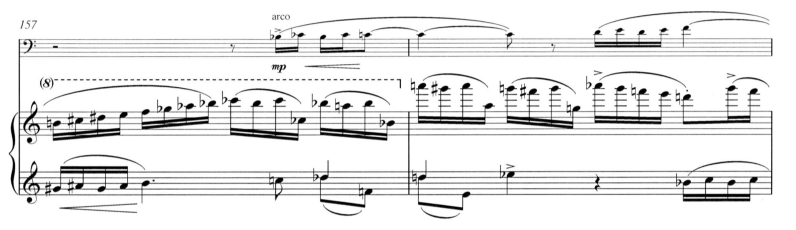

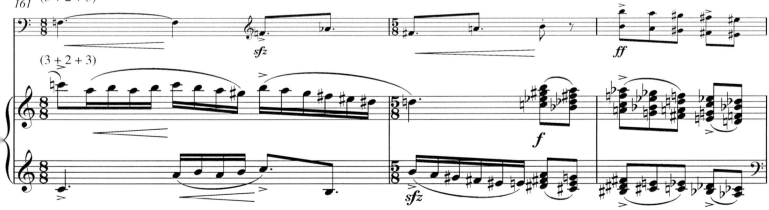

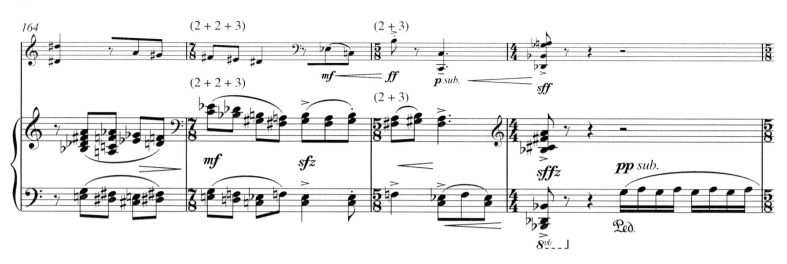

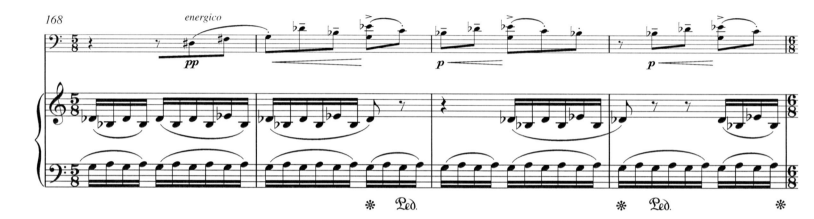

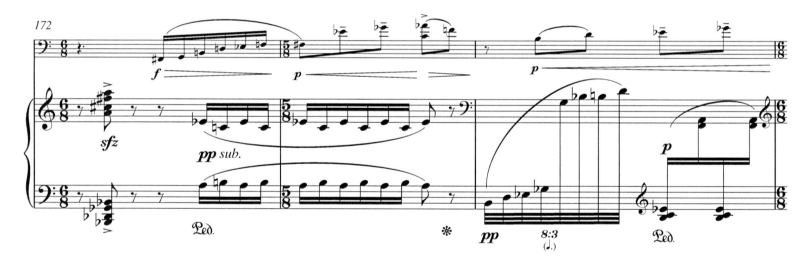

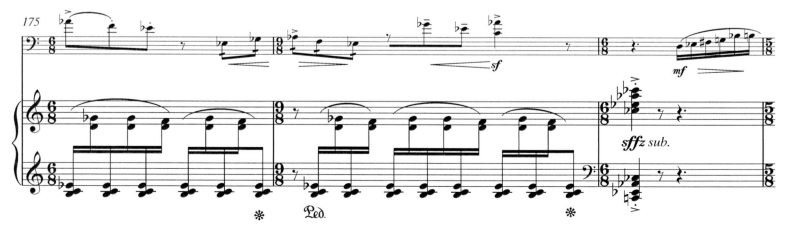

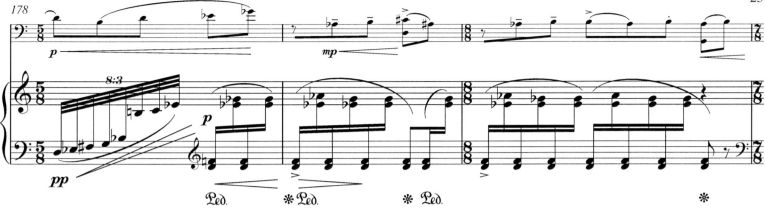

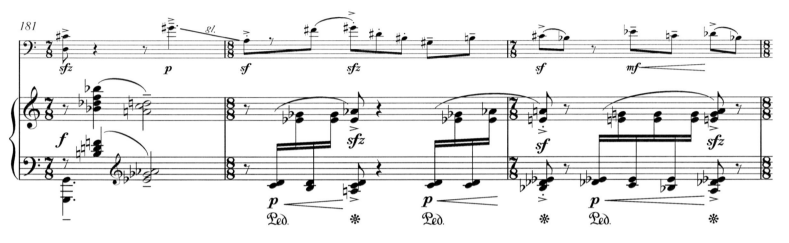

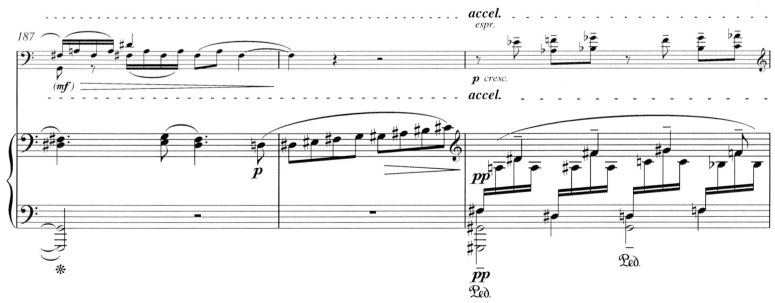

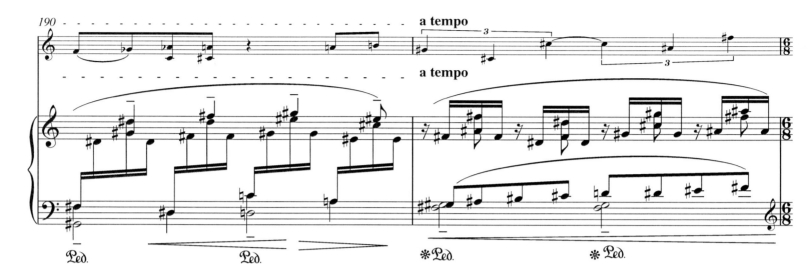

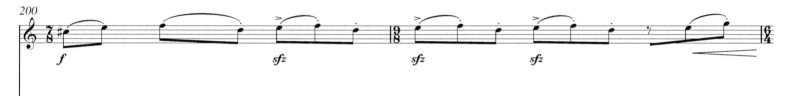

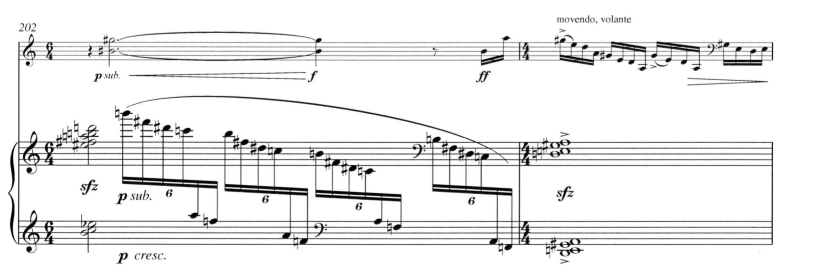

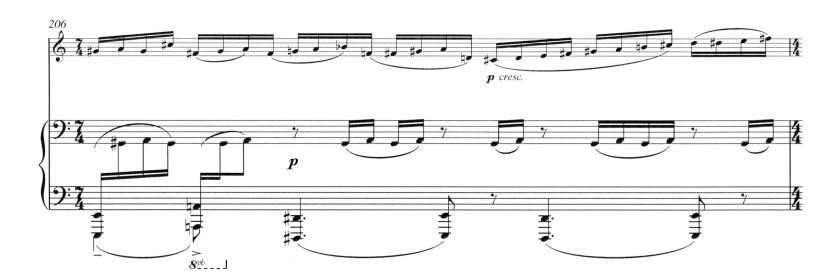

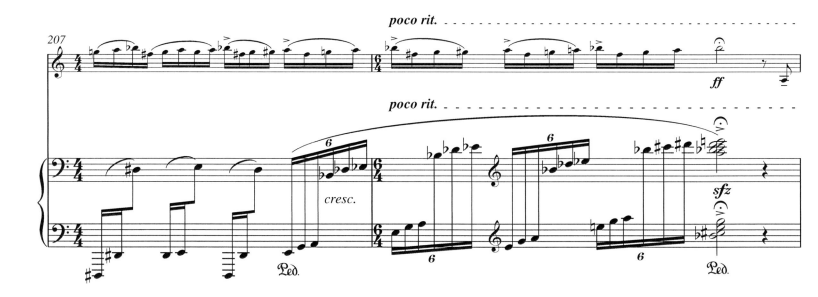

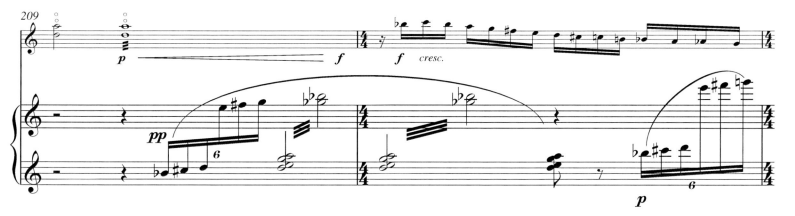

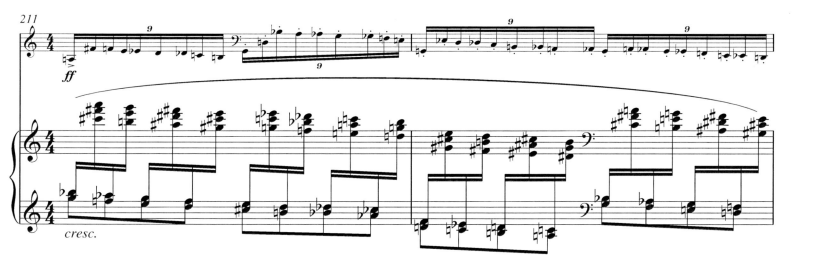